Original title:
Living Between the Rooms

Copyright © 2025 Creative Arts Management OÜ
All rights reserved.

Author: Henry Beaumont
ISBN HARDBACK: 978-1-80587-128-6
ISBN PAPERBACK: 978-1-80587-598-7

Navigating Silent Halls

In the halls where echoes play,
I trip on thoughts that slip away.
With shoes that squeak and socks askew,
I dance like no one sees me do.

Around each corner, shadows creep,
A cat rehearses, or so it seems.
I chuckle at the walls that sigh,
And wonder if they ever try.

The lights flicker, what's the game?
A ghostly friend who knows my name?
I wave hello, it waves goodbye,
Our secret joke, just us and shy.

With every step, the past will tease,
An ice cream cone, a sneeze, a breeze.
I laugh aloud at what I find,
This quirky maze, it warps the mind.

Whispered Conversations in the Void

In rooms where whispers float like dust,
I chat with chairs and stir the rust.
The curtains gossip, secrets unfold,
Tales of the brave and tales of the bold.

A shoe left behind, a sock that trips,
I ponder the world on its silly flips.
The fridge hums softly, a tune from yore,
While I debate if milk's still score.

My thoughts bounce high off ceiling beams,
Each creak and crack relays my dreams.
A toaster nods at things divine,
And laughs at crumbs left by design.

With every laugh, I find my groove,
In this silent dance, I just can't move.
What fun it is, to be a blur,
In whispered realms where dreams confer.

Between the Walls of Change

When walls start quaking with every cheer,
I ponder if they're hiding fear.
A clock ticks loudly, tick tock, it grins,
Where laughter hides, a mischief spins.

Cushions conspire with a sly old cat,
They summon up a chat about the mat.
Do they plan to start a pillow fight?
Or stage a coup in the middle of night?

The pictures watch with silent ease,
As I trip over my own left knee.
A door swings open with playful glee,
Inviting me to join the spree.

In the hallways of yesteryears, I roam,
Where whispers giggle and chaos is home.
It's a circus show, a merry play,
Between changes where I gleefully sway.

The Quiet Corridor

In the corridor where silence sings,
I juggle thoughts like playful things.
With every step, the floorboards creak,
I snicker at the secrets they speak.

A hallway stretches, long and bright,
As shadows tease and take their flight.
A broom stands guard, a sentinel bold,
It sweeps my jokes, or so I'm told.

Posters smile, their colors gleam,
An artful chat spills out like cream.
I wink at windows, they blink back light,
This corridor feels just right tonight.

With every twist and tiny turn,
Life's little lessons, I gladly learn.
In this corridor, I find my cue,
To laugh, to cheer, and feel anew.

Twilight Between the Walls

In twilight's glow, I roam and peep,
The shadows dance, while secrets creep.
A sock lost here, a shoe misplaced,
This home's a maze, I'll never waste.

Pillows chat and cushions sigh,
The lamp debates if it should cry.
As fridge's hum becomes my tune,
I chuckle with the sneaky broom.

My cat's the king of this estate,
He rules the chaos, checks the fate.
In every room a mystery lies,
This puzzle's fun, oh what a prize!

A cup of tea, a slice of pie,
I wave goodbye to the world outside.
In this odd home, with laughter loud,
I'll enjoy life, unbowed and proud.

Solace in the Gaps

Between these walls, a world abounds,
I find my peace, in laughter's sounds.
The fridge hums jokes beneath its door,
While dust bunnies dance on the floor.

Cobwebs spin tales of secret lives,
Where mischief brews and humor thrives.
Lost in the seams of softest light,
I giggle with the socks at night.

The kettle sings, a merry tune,
It knows my heart, a trusty boon.
With every slip of the daring cat,
I burst in laughter, imagine that!

So here I stay, my cozy space,
With quirks and quirrks, I fondly trace.
In these small gaps, I find great cheer,
A home of joy, I hold so dear.

The Gap of Unraveled Dreams

In corners tucked, dreams sway and spin,
Like a dog chasing its own tail's grin.
There's humor in the mess I share,
Between the dreams, I giggle and stare.

A stack of books, all askew,
Whisper secrets; oh, how they grew!
With every flip, there's laughter's sound,
Unraveled tales, joy tightly wound.

Those mismatched socks sit side by side,
In a world where sense has surely died.
Their journey is a riotous quest,
In this odd trip, I'm truly blessed.

So let them lay, these crazy schemes,
For here I roam through tangled dreams.
Each twist and turn, a laugh, a cheer,
In every gap, my heart draws near.

The Cornerstone of Ambivalence

In the corner, my chair sits still,
Half undecided, loves to thrill.
To nap or read? What a game,
This throne of chaos, never tame.

Cushions bicker; who knows the best?
The coffee pot, it laughs the rest.
Between my thoughts, both here and there,
I ponder while I flip my hair.

Books might argue, but I just grin,
In this sweet mess, I find my win.
The clock strikes loud, I tilt my head,
Time's a jester, dancing instead.

So here I sit, in blissful doubt,
With my quirky crew, without a pout.
In every twist, a chuckle found,
My life's a joke, spinning around.

Halls of a Forgotten Mind

In the hallway of yonder thought,
Where socks and ideas often fought,
Hats hang low, like dreams unsaid,
I trip on a memory, bump my head.

Closets housing ghosts with flair,
Old treasures lost in dusty air,
An old chair whispers tales so bold,
While I search for my keys, thirty times old.

The fridge hums a sleepy song,
While that leftover pizza feels so wrong,
I ponder snacks that could set me free,
But I can't decide, oh, what could it be?

A mirror cracks with laughter's plea,
Reflecting the chaos that lives in me,
In this house of giggles and half-forgot,
I embrace the silly, the tangled knot.

Unraveled Threads of Being

In the tapestry of time, I weave,
A sock that's lonely, a sight to grieve,
Buttons pop like thoughts unplanned,
As I aim for grace but land unplanned.

Curtains flutter with gossip tight,
Whispers of what was lost to night,
The cat sits smug on a pile of yarn,
While I wrestle with laundry's true charm.

Stairs ascend to nowhere grand,
Each creak, a giggle, the floorboards stand,
I chase my thoughts, but they run away,
In laughter's realm, I choose to stay.

A hat sits crooked in the breeze,
With every step, I trip with ease,
Unraveling life with a playful twist,
In this whimsical world, I can't resist.

The In-Between Journey

Between the meals, adventures sprout,
Sandwiches waiting, no jokes about,
I take a trip down the hallway bright,
To find snacks that give me true delight.

Footsteps dance on the spotty mat,
When I grab a treat and hear my cat,
A sudden chase ensues with glee,
As I dodge furniture, wild and free.

In the living room, a sock parade,
Dandelion seeds, all charades made,
As I tumble past the old TV,
I laugh at myself, just let it be.

Through the dining room, I sneak and peek,
Find crumbs of laughter, that's what I seek,
With every turn, a new delight,
In a game of hide-and-seek all night.

Quietude of the Overlooked

In the corners where shadows play,
Are treasures hiding, come what may,
Dust bunnies hop with a wink and grin,
Whispering secrets where they've been.

Underneath the couch, socks unite,
Old toys cavort in a foam delight,
As the clock ticks, sounds of a jest,
In the quietude, I find my zest.

Walls adorned with fading lines,
Mismatched artwork, stories entwined,
A half-eaten donut sits on the stand,
Waiting patiently for my hand.

Between the whispers and half-heard guides,
I stroll through moments, where laughter resides,
Finding joy in the overlooked scene,
In the quietude, I reign as queen.

Intersection of Echoes

In a hallway where laughter skips,
The echoes trip over clumsy lips.
A cat in a bow tie struts with flair,
As socks come to life, dancing in pairs.

And the fridge hums a tune so jolly,
While leftovers plot their next big folly.
A spoon winks at a fork with a grin,
Saying, 'Let's dish out some chaos again!'

Portals of Possibility

A closet that leads to a land of socks,
Where dust bunnies weave into silly flocks.
The lampshade's a crown on a chair of fame,
In the kingdom of clutter, all share the same name.

A mirror reflects a dance of delay,
As mops form a chorus in their own cabaret.
With every turn of a door's squeaky heel,
New adventures await, that's the real deal!

When Walls Speak Softly

Whispers drift through the wallpaper cracks,
Telling tales of the dog who loves snacks.
In the corners, the shadows play hide and seek,
While the clock chuckles softly, ticking antique.

The ceiling fans gossip with a gentle spin,
About wild parties where no one's been.
With each wall painting a story so bright,
Who knew that drywall could be such a delight?

The Uncharted Territories

Under the couch lurks a treasure trove,
Where missing remotes and odd socks rove.
An empire of crumbs, the carrot brigade,
Plotting a coup that may never fade.

Through the curtains, the sun spills its beans,
On the shenanigans made by mischievous machines.
In corners unexplored, giggles abound,
In this wacky world where joy knows no bound.

Reflections of Possible Futures

In the kitchen, dreams collide,
The toaster sings, my bread's fried.
I ponder what the fridge might say,
If only it weren't my snack buffet.

The cat debates with my shoe,
On whose next nap is overdue.
The couch is plotting a new scheme,
To hold the weight of my wildest dream.

A dance-off with the dust bunnies,
My only rivals for all these funnies.
The calendar laughs at tomorrow's plight,
As I dress up in pajamas so tight.

I glance out the window for straight answers,
But all I see are sunlit prancers.
With life's absurd twists, oh what a ride,
In this whimsical world where I confide.

The Interlude's Harmony

A slice of cake, a moment's bliss,
Caught between chaos and quietness.
The phone rings loud, it's Auntie May,
With gossip that will lead me astray.

I hum a tune while dusting my plans,
The vacuum loudly plays in bands.
A fortune cookie whispers to me,
'Today, you'll laugh—just wait and see!'

In the laundry, colors collide,
As socks complain of mismatched pride.
The blender's symphony whirrs away,
Making smoothies of my dismay.

Outside the window, squirrels compete,
For acorns and the title of elite.
They chatter tales of nutty schemes,
While I sip dreams in my dozing themes.

A Stillness at the Edge

On the balcony, a potted joke,
The plant insists I take a poke.
I swear it winked just yesterday,
But who am I to disobey?

The wind plays harp with my hair a-fly,
As I chase shadows that skip by.
A bird swoops in, loud and bold,
Singing secrets of old I'm told.

A knock at the door—a pizza surprise,
With toppings that make my taste buds rise.
The takeout menu's a thrilling read,
And life becomes an epic feed.

Here on the ledge, I find my place,
Between the giggles and the grace.
The stillness holds a laughable dream,
As thoughts escape like whipped cream.

The Color of Silence

In a touch of quiet, the walls might chat,
The paint's too pink, or is it that?
I listen for whispers from the chair,
But it just creaks with empty air.

The rug's a colorful wild affair,
With stories woven with flair.
A sock puppet stands, ready to brawl,
Debating over dust, not much at all.

In the stillness, my thoughts bounce high,
As paper airplanes take to the sky.
They glide through silence, leaving a trace,
Of spontaneous laughter across my face.

The clock ticks loud, a metronome's play,
Marking moments like a clumsy ballet.
In hues of silence, what a delight,
Finding joy in the hush and the light.

Where Light and Shadow Converge

In this corner, I'm a dancer,
Where dust bunnies waltz with chance.
The light flickers like a prancer,
And shadows join in a silly dance.

I tiptoe past the drawn-up shades,
With socks that could start a riot.
My cat thinks he's a knight with blades,
I'm just hoping he keeps quiet.

The fridge hums a lonely tune,
While the clock laughs at my plight.
This late-night snack's a happy moon,
I might sleepwalk into the light.

So here I straddle giggle and gloom,
For all of life's strange little quirks.
In every room, there's ample room,
With laughter lurking in the works.

Fragments of an Unfinished Tale

Between my dreams and morning's light,
A sock escapes, oh what a sight!
He hides and seeks, laughs in delight,
While I chase legends, lost in plight.

Old stories lurk in dusty nooks,
My books call me, with crooked looks.
Each page a world where mischief cooks,
Tea parties sprout from flimsy hooks.

The coffee brews a bumpy ride,
I spill a bit, the cat's my guide.
We journey far, my mug and I,
In search of tales that seem to fly.

These fragments dance, they twist and twirl,
In half-lit rooms, they leap and whirl.
With every drop, a whimsy pearl,
A quirky life begins to unfurl.

The Quietude Between Walls

In the stillness, whispers play,
The curtain flirts with breezy sway.
I hear the clock, its prankster way,
Telling tales of yesterday.

A gnome decorates the ledge,
Mischief sparkles in his eyes.
He waves at me, a solemn pledge,
To keep me laughing through the sighs.

Footsteps echo like a song,
But only I can hum along.
In this quiet, feels so wrong,
Yet every day, I break the gong.

With pots and pans as my duet,
Cooking up mischief, no regret.
This harmony, a silly fret,
In every pause, new laughter set.

Embracing the Overlaps

Like puzzle pieces, here we stand,
In a tangle that's subtly planned.
The dog has chewed through my band,
While socks declare war on the land.

I wear mismatched shoes like a pro,
Each step's a guess, a comedic show.
Will I trip or glide, who knows?
Adventure's here, come join the flow!

The windows tell tales when they creak,
Of knock-knock jokes and hide-and-seek.
I raise a finger, say, "No sneak!"
In every overlap, there's a peak.

So here we sit, in chaos grand,
Where every corner makes a stand.
Life's a giggle we've planned,
In the overlaps, together we band.

Serenade of the In-Between

In a hallway where socks often stray,
Echoes of laughter come out to play.
A dance with the dust bunnies, all in good fun,
Chasing misplaced keys 'til the day is done.

The fridge hums a song, a cool serenade,
While jars of old pickles are boldly displayed.
The sofa's a throne of forgotten delight,
Comfy and messy, it welcomes the night.

A spilled cup of coffee joins in the jest,
While mismatched cushions provide perfect rest.
Who needs a stage when the world's such a mess?
Here in the chaos, we find happiness.

So raise up a glass to the snacks in the bowl,
And toast to the chaos that fills up the hole.
For in every nook, a secret resides,
In this whimsical life, our joy safely hides.

Palettes of Possibility

In corners where crayons and papers collide,
Sketches of dreams in a colorful slide.
A splatter of paint on the wall is a find,
Reminds us of giggles and silliness combined.

Balancing the broom on a toe with great flair,
Echoes of mischief dance through the air.
Mismatched socks tell tales of laundry gone wrong,
The art of the in-between is where we belong.

The ceiling fan spins a whimsical tale,
Catching the laughter that starts to prevail.
Shadows of pets take shape in delight,
Acrobats' leaps in the encompassing night.

So gather your colors, let imagination thrive,
In a world where the oddities help us survive.
For every dull corner is simply a chance,
To turn up the fun and join in the dance!

Edges Where Shadows Play

In the corners, where shadows like to sneak,
A tickle of giggles is what we seek.
The cat chases light with a pounce and a dash,
While dust motes waltz in a sparkly clash.

A rug beneath toes holds stories untold,
Of trips and mishaps and daringly bold.
With every sneaky step, laughter's invite,
Adventure awaits in the dimness of night.

Behind every curtain, a secret resides,
Where socks have been hiding with nothing to hide.
The maze of our lives twists and twirls all around,
But in the tight corners, true fun can be found.

So let's not forget the joy in the stray,
In the edges where shadows tumble and play.
A chuckle, a sneeze, or a tip of the hat,
Life's best surprises come from moments like that!

Fragments of Solitude

In the quiet of corners, where whispers reside,
A sock takes a nap, and the cat's eyes confide.
With tea stains as artwork, we sip and we sigh,
   Life's little odd ducks flutter joyfully by.

The chair creaks a tune, a soft serenade,
  As half-finished puzzles begin to invade.
Each piece tells a story, hilarious and bright,
Of battles with crumbs in the fridge overnight.

Post-its and doodles cover the fridge,
Ideas come flooding over each ridge.
A castle of solitude perfectly made,
Where giggles and chocolate in tandem invade.

So here's to the fragments that make up our days,
Between laughter and chaos, in colorful ways.
In the hush of quiet, we dance with our dreams,
Finding joy in the fragments, or so it seems.

The Unseen Connections

In the hallway, I find a shoe,
Its partner's missing, who knew?
Tangled wires beneath the bed,
My cat's new toy, or a snack instead?

Chairs that wobble, stories to tell,
One's a throne, the other a shell.
Sock puppets formed with flair,
Imaginings dance through the air.

A dust bunny leaps, a hopscotch game,
Each sweep of the broom, adds to its fame.
Paintings ask, "Where have you been?"
Laughing at memories, tucked in between.

From closet to kitchen, the echoes play,
Thoughts wander, then scamper away.
Yet in these corners we find our cheer,
Life's wacky moments draw us near.

Driftwood Between Spaces

A coat on the chair, a hat on the shelf,
They plan a party, all by themselves.
The fridge hums a tune, off-key but bright,
Dancing leftovers under the moonlight.

My slippers stage a daring race,
To the couch, oh what a place!
Coffee spills in an artful flare,
Masterpieces made with flair and care.

The bathroom mirror holds secrets galore,
Reflections of laughter, and who knows what more?
Shampoo bottles gossip, sharing their tales,
While rubber ducks plot with silly gales.

But wait, where's my other sock?
The dryer's a mystery, a black hole clock.
Yet between the spaces, I'll hardly frown,
For each oddity wears a smile, not a crown.

Navigating the Gaps

Between the sofa and side table there's a crack,
Where lost remotes seem to hatch a scheme,
They plan their great escape, it seems quite clear,
To join the dust bunnies on their sweet frontier.

The fridge hums low, a lazy old tune,
As milk nags the cheese—it's all over too soon.
Spilled cereal makes a crunchy landscape,
Oh, breakfast adventures, give me a cape!

Chairs stacked high, they're plotting a coup,
In the stillness, they giggle, oh what a view!
Each pillow holds dreams of wild, playful flights,
As curtains whisper secrets of long, cozy nights.

Between each gap, a laughter-filled space,
Gathering quirks, a warm embrace.
With each little quirk, we proudly dance,
In this peculiar home, we take our chance.

The Silent Passage

In the hallway, echoes echo loud,
Chasing each other, forming a crowd.
Curtains flutter, having their say,
Whispering stories in a playful way.

Socks unite behind the couch,
A love story told by a mouse.
The kettle sings, a melodious treat,
Holding court, it can't be beat.

Books on the shelf, in secret chats,
Sharing tales about jazzy hats.
Bookmarks are mischievous, hanging around,
While pages rustle, they're lost and found.

But in this passage, time's a sly thief,
Collecting our moments, both joy and grief.
Yet laughter softens each twist and bend,
In this quiet journey, we find a friend.

Inhabiting the Air Between

In corners where shadows play,
Two mismatched socks lead the way.
A dance of dust bunnies takes flight,
As I sip tea with a ghostly sprite.

I trip on a thought that forgot to bloom,
While laughter echoes within the room.
The cat gives a wink, as if on cue,
With tales of mischief that once rang true.

The Undefined Spaces

In the crack where the wall meets the floor,
Lie secrets of socks, and more folklore.
The fridge hums a tune, a curious song,
While half-eaten pizza claims it's not wrong.

There's a fortune in crumbs beneath the chair,
As I discover that I'm not quite aware.
The dust motes dance like a comical crew,
While I ponder if yesterday's waffles were two.

Limbo of Forgotten Roads

In the hallway where echoes go to sleep,
Dusty memories begin to creep.
A shoe that's lost its partner in crime,
Tells jokes of adventure, trapped in time.

The visit from the vacuum's a running joke,
While lightbulbs flicker like some old bloke.
With each passing minute, I find my place,
In this realm of chaos, I've made my space.

The Silence That Binds

In the pause between laughter and sighs,
Ghosts of the past wage comical cries.
A door that creaks like it's telling tales,
Of misfit adventures and runaway snails.

The clock ticks loud, yet time slips away,
As I ponder the meaning of socks in dismay.
Each giggle escapes like a mischievous sprite,
In the silence that binds, everything feels light.

The Quiet Intersections

In corners where silence plays,
Two socks converse in funny ways.
A cat naps on the narrow beam,
While curtains plot their grand daydreams.

The fridge hums jokes from the past,
As crumbs hold meetings, quite steadfast.
A broom leans close, whispers and sighs,
Forgotten dust bunnies plan their rise.

Cushions gather for gossip galore,
Trading tales from the kitchen floor.
The clock rolls its eyes, ticks slow like a snail,
While the phone rings laughter, a comical tale.

Amid playful shadows, life unfolds,
In subtle antics, secrets told.
A dance of daily quirks, so sweet,
Where joy pretends to take a seat.

Melodies in Midair

The spoons join hands in a silver band,
While the forks tap dance on the counter stand.
A kettle whistles a silly tune,
As teabags plot to dance by the moon.

An old guitar rests, quietly bemused,
While the chairs make plans, slightly confused.
Each step is a rhythm, a jolly parade,
In the spaces, a ruckus is lovingly made.

The lightbulbs wink like stars on cue,
Casting shadows of jokes, bright and anew.
A broomstick rides on a whimsical flight,
As the dust motes twirl in soft delight.

In every crevice, a chuckle is found,
As laughter echoes, spinning around.
In rooms where the silence is filled with cheer,
Magic happens when friends are near.

The Hidden Narrative

Between the walls, a secret's spun,
Where socks find laughter, always on the run.
The mop tells tales of floors once slick,
While the dust smiles, feeling quite slick.

Under the sofa, a saga unfolds,
As toys debate their fortunes bold.
A rug rolls over, tucking its edges tight,
Creating knots of humor, day and night.

The calendar winks, flipping past the days,
Hiding punchlines in its mundane ways.
Each tick of the clock spins laughter in air,
While the pantry whispers secrets with flair.

In these moments, the ordinary gleams,
With quirky narratives spun in dreams.
Life tiptoes lightly, chasing the loom,
In every breath, a tip-toe of room!

Beyond the Veil of Normalcy

In the kitchen, socks do a jig,
Eggs are dancing in the pan, so big.
Bread sings ballads on the shelf,
While I try to be a normal self.

The cat's wearing my favorite hat,
While the dog contemplates a chat.
Down the hall, the fridge hums a tune,
As if it knows we're all cartooned.

Mirrors show reflections askew,
Where everyone looks like you-know-who.
Lamps flicker like they're in a rave,
Who knew lights had a life to crave?

Beyond sanity's playful edge,
Lies a world that loves to hedge.
With every step, a laugh may spring,
In the mundane dance, feel the zing!

The Room That Isn't

There's a room that's never found,
With a carpet of clouds and a wall that's sound.
Chairs made of whispers, tables of dust,
In this playful place, reason is a bust.

I knocked once, but it giggled back,
Finding doorways in the paper stack.
Floors made of jello, ceilings of cheer,
The more I explore, the less I'm here.

A window shows a world upside down,
Where the sun wears a frown, and stars wear a crown.
I sip on a drink that turns into dreams,
In this silly place, nothing's as it seems.

The clock chimed backward, and oh what fun,
Time threw a party when no one could run.
In the room that isn't, let's never part,
For in its nonsense, lies a clever heart.

Shadows of Uncertainty

Shadows dance with a rogue's delight,
Whispering secrets of wrong and right.
They play hopscotch on the floor's wide space,
Leaving behind smiles in their trace.

A shadow cat stalks a shadow dog,
While I trip over a whimsical log.
What's in the cupboard? It's hard to tell,
Maybe broccoli or a wishing well?

Dancing doubts wear a polka-dot dress,
While hopes parade, looking for success.
Each shape mutters a playful jest,
In the haze of invisible quests.

So here we stand, on wobbly ground,
With shadows making mirth all around.
In this realm of giggles and sighs,
Let's find the fun where uncertainty lies.

An Odyssey of Interlude

Here begins the epic on the couch,
With potato chips and a squeaky grouch.
Remote in hand, I sail through the day,
Navigating shows in a comical way.

Snacks are my crew, popcorn waves ahoy,
Charting new courses with each silly ploy.
Through channels of laughter and maps of cheer,
Every episode shouts, 'Adventure is near!'

A plot twist whirls, and I giggle hard,
As my socks declare war in the yard.
Characters jump from screen to the floor,
In this odyssey, fun is never a bore.

So let's hoist the flag of laughter and roam,
In this vivid interlude we call home.
With every moment crafted absurdly right,
Here's to our journey—a whimsical flight!

The Interstitial Journey

In a gap where socks do hide,
I dance like I'm on a fun slide.
The fridge hums a secret tune,
While I'm lost in a midday swoon.

Chasing crumbs on the kitchen wall,
I trip over the cat, oh what a fall!
Each corner holds another quirk,
As I wander like I'm on a lark.

Spilling things, it's a balmy breeze,
As the phone rings, I spill my peas.
My slippers squeak like a squeaky toy,
Each moment is a spark of joy.

So here I thrive in this little space,
Where chaos turns to sheer embrace.
In the nooks I find my bliss,
With laughter wrapped in socks amiss.

Moments in the Margins

On the edge of the sofa's arm,
I find a comic's silly charm.
The world rushes in a busy race,
I'm here with popcorn, in my place.

Wobbling on a stack of books,
I spy on my neighbors with silly looks.
Each glance invites a riotous laugh,
Absurdity in the margins' path.

With unmade beds my daily throne,
Here's where imagination is grown.
Between two pillows, I dream wide,
In a fortress where giggles reside.

I open the door to a new delight,
Where socks and giggles blend just right.
Filling spaces with careless cheer,
Creating memories year after year.

Clarity in the Crack Between

In the crevice of the couch I peek,
Finding a cookie, it's quite the treat!
Dust bunnies whisper their tiny tales,
As I daydream about epic fails.

Under the bed, I catch some shoes,
Where monsters might just snooze and snooze.
Eccentric worlds in a lost remote,
Floating boats made of notes I wrote.

A pillow fort stands tall and proud,
Protecting me from the bustling crowd.
With spaghetti strings as my guiding line,
I craft a meal that's truly divine!

Here laughter echoes, a playful song,
In whispers of 'what could go wrong?'
Each crack becomes a canvas bright,
Where mischief dances in soft twilight.

Transience of the In-Betweens

Between the door and the table's edge,
I'm part-time king on a crumpled ledge.
Finding treasures of forgotten snack,
Adjusted chairs, I launch my crack.

The light flips and shadows play,
As I jiggle on my knees, hooray!
Moments linger in curious spaces,
Creating smiles on all our faces.

With chairs stacked high like a crazy game,
I reclaim the air in my glory frame.
Sprinkling giggles on the floor,
As I pretend it's a dance encore!

In these in-betweens I find my tune,
Where time eludes like a laughing moon.
Each little crack, a comedy show,
As I embrace the chaos in a warm glow.

Threshold Whispers

At the door, I pause and peek,
A sock dropped here, a shoe so chic.
The cat spies ghosts on the stair,
Sassy whispers fill the air.

Between the rooms, a dance begins,
Mismatched socks are now our sins.
I trip on toys, I laugh and sway,
Why is laundry always in the way?

My fridge hums, a gossip queen,
Telling secrets of what you've seen.
The vacuum sneaks, a ninja bold,
Cleaning up secrets, oh, so old.

A thumbtack dreams of higher aims,
While brushes ponder timeless games.
A keyhole winks, just look, you'll find,
A world that giggles, oh so kind.

Ghosts of the Hallway

Two lamps argue on either side,
Laughing at shadows they can't abide.
Mismatched cousins in strange attire,
Whispering tales of their lost desire.

The hallway's a stage, we take our bows,
With echoes that tickle, we can't say how.
The mailman's sock staggers on by,
A ghost in the middle of a pie in the sky.

Doorbells ring with rusty tones,
Poltergeist cats steal the bones.
Stairs become slides on a whim,
Where laughter's the sport, and the lights get dim.

Invisible friends pull at my coat,
As I hustle through, like a runaway boat.
In this quirky space, oddities play,
Even the dust bunnies have something to say.

Echoes in the Interstice

In the gap where silence breeds,
A rubber duck dreams of grand feats.
It squeaks to the mop in a fit of glee,
'We're the best team, just you wait and see!'

The laundry sings a tuneful fight,
With shirts that twirl into the night.
The towels cheer on, a fluffy crew,
With every spin, they're up for a view.

I fetch a snack from the cupboard deep,
And find a cookie, then take a leap.
The shelves are brimming with oddities bold,
Nuts that crack jokes, and bolts of gold.

In this quirky nook, we sway and swing,
With echoes of laughter that always cling.
Unruly furniture joins in the spree,
Who needs a ghost when it's all so free?

Secrets in the Spaces

In corners lush with dust and dreams,
We spy on socks with pretty seams.
The chair sits grumpy, a sage so wise,
While out from the cushions, a sneaky surprise!

The blender gossips with pots and pans,
Swapping tales of wild food plans.
Fridge magnets tease, a colorful crew,
Drawing doodles of things they can't do.

A mouse in the wall hums a tune,
While shadows whirl by, over the moon.
Pillows are pondering, soft and round,
Every secret here is delightfully sound.

The clock ticks laughter, a merry sound,
In this laughter-laden, playful ground.
With every step, a giggle blooms,
Oh, the charm of our quirky rooms!

Eclipsed Views on the Horizon

A cat naps near the chair,
Dreaming of places far away.
My sock's lost its pair,
Wandering into yesterday.

A fridge hums with a tune,
While cereal waits in a bowl.
I ponder the shape of the moon,
As I search for my lost role.

The doors creak with great flair,
Like they're auditioning for a play.
I laugh at the dust in the air,
Capping off another odd day.

Here I dance on a line,
Between snacks and some dreams.
Life's a comic design,
Bursting out at the seams.

The Unfolding of Essence

A knock on the wall,
Was it the neighbor or a ghost?
I shout, 'Where's my ball?'
And it echoes like a boast.

The toaster giggles on cue,
As bread begins to rise.
I pretend I'm a chef on a view,
With my culinary disguise.

My plants join the fun,
Swaying slightly in the breeze.
I swear they've begun,
To plot against my cheese.

Between flavors and scents,
Life is a quirky affair.
With each little event,
I laugh out loud in mid-air.

Stirrings in the In-Between

The clock ticks like a prude,
Counting down my snack time.
I feel a bit subdued,
Doodling lyrics in mime.

A suitcase smiles so bright,
It's ready for escape.
But I'll stay in for the night,
With popcorn and my cape.

A chair spins in delight,
Its fate is in the air.
I'm caught in the twilight,
Waiting for a joke to share.

In the corners, secrets creep,
Juggling thoughts like a clown.
I giggle and I leap,
Before the sun goes down.

The Unseen Thread

Invisible strings pull tight,
I dangle like some yarn.
Is that a cat in the night?
Or just my laundry's charm?

I juggle thoughts like plates,
While balancing on one shoe.
Even this giggle elongates,
As reality bids adieu.

Amid the chaos and spree,
An echo of laughter grows.
Like hidden eyes I can't see,
Catching all of my woes.

Each nook hides a tale,
From tickles to cloudy days.
In this odd little trail,
Life dances in quirky ways.

Whispers of What Could Be

In the hall, I trip and sway,
The cat laughs as I delay.
Thoughts of snacks float like air,
Should I stay or just declare?

Couch potato dreams arise,
Should I nap or socialize?
The remote calls with sweet allure,
Yet, friend texted, "Come and tour!"

Socks in odd pairs, where do they roam?
In this maze, I feel at home.
Chasing visions, who knows what's next?
My life's a sitcom, awkwardly perplexed.

The Detailed Interstice

In the kitchen, crumbs parade,
I cook, but what's the trade?
Spices dance, they tease and twirl,
Oops, not enough to make it swirl.

The fridge hums a quirky tune,
Leftovers grinning like a cartoon.
Dinner plans burst like a bubble,
Why's the pantry full of trouble?

Sipping tea, I ponder deep,
In my thoughts, both bliss and sheep.
Here's a note that says, 'Just breathe,'
But next door, they're planting seeds.

Where Ambiguous Moments Dwell

From the hallway, echoes gleam,
I hear my neighbor's dream.
A toaster pops; we shan't forget,
In the chaos, we're all set.

Eccentric laughter fills the air,
Who knew three cats could cause such flair?
Juggling chores or maybe fun,
In this maze, I've just begun.

A hiccup here, a giggle there,
Amid the chaos, we share a dare.
Sticky notes of half-baked plans,
Life's rich tapestry made by hands.

Portraits of the Interstitial

Caught in the space 'twixt room and dream,
I sketch my life, a comic theme.
With coffee cups in disarray,
Each mix-up brightens my gray.

Roommates' snoring like a band,
Their wild tales, I can't withstand.
A mop that dances on its own,
This home's a place I've overgrown.

Fights with furniture, or so it seems,
Brush my hand across the beams.
Adventure stirs in every crack,
In these spaces, I'll not look back.

The Delicate Balance of Being

In the kitchen, I'm a chef,
In the living room, a king.
But in the hall, I just can't tell,
If I'm more of a jester or a string.

Dining on thoughts of what to do,
Juggling chores like a circus clown.
But in that space in between my tasks,
I quietly question, "Am I upside down?"

On the couch, I'm the master of art,
My snacks arranged like a Picasso's chart.
Yet step through the door, and with a start,
I find my socks have declared a revolt on their part.

But laughter echoes in each little nook,
As I wander through each room, just like a book.
And even when chaos begins to cook,
I dance in the mess, like a tangle of good luck.

Threads of Continuity

With spaghetti on my shirt, I proclaim,
"Dinner's an exhibition of my wild fame."
But in the hallway, I lose my way,
As socks get tangled in my playful game.

Cups and plates, a warrior's quest,
Battle on surfaces, who gets the best?
Yet moving to the bedroom, I'll confess,
It's just me and my thoughts, sharing a jest.

Between the world of snacks and sleep,
Lurks the dust bunny with secrets to keep.
But hey, I'm a hero in my own sweep,
As I navigate life with a tireless leap.

What a ride, from room to room,
Like a sitcom starring chaos, there's always room.
And in every in-between, I'll make it bloom,
Creating laughter in a juggling gloom.

Echoes in the Overlap

Where the living meets the dining, there's a ruckus,
As I meditate on muffins amidst all the fuss.
In the bathroom, I ponder the meaning of it,
While my rubber ducky gives philosophical tips.

Here in the hallway, shoe battles commence,
Pairing lefts with rights—what a nonsense suspense!
And as I chat with my plants, they all say,
"We're not judging, just hoping for some rain repence."

In corners where echoes bounce like a ball,
I find a lost sock—oh look, it's tall!
Yet in that confounding overlap of space,
I can't help but laugh at the humorous hall.

But really, life's just one big silly jig,
From kitchen to bedroom, oh what a gig!
I'll laugh with the echoes, I won't be a twig,
Dancing between the chaos, life's grand sprig.

The Stillness Between Waves

As I stand at the door, there's a quiet sensation,
Between waves of chaos, I find a vacation.
With toys on the floor like a bumpy shore,
I laugh at this stillness, it's a strange kind of creation.

Like a surfboard I ride on the tide of my time,
In the midst of the laundry, I find my prime.
Folding mismatched socks, it feels like a climb,
But each little victory is suddenly sublime.

A dog on my lap, a cat in the air,
I balance the circus with a humorous flair.
In that stillness between what's scattered everywhere,
I giggle as I tiptoe, walking on air.

So let's raise a glass to the gaps in our days,
And embrace the odd moments, in our own quirky ways.
For it's all about fun in this life's endless maze,
With laughter on the edge of the waves that we blaze.

Between Memories and Dreams

I tiptoe through the hall of time,
Where socks can hold a secret rhyme.
Each forgotten snack, a joyful tune,
Caught between a fork and spoon.

The laundry basket sings my name,
While dust bunnies plot their game.
I chase the cat in shadowed light,
While he judges my crown of fright.

Echoes of laughter bounce and play,
As I search for lost keys, come what may.
The fridge hums stories I can't tell,
Of midnight snacks that, oh so well!

So here I dance in twilight's glow,
Where memories bloom and mischief flows.
I'll just pretend that all is fine,
As I sip my soda—how divine!

The Quiet Inhabitants

In a chair that's lost its spring,
I find the ghosts of everything.
A gnome with eyes, oh so wide,
Whispers secrets—the couch's pride.

The clock ticks on with such a grin,
While dust speaks softly—where to begin?
It says, 'Who needs to leave this place?,'
As I rummage with a puzzled face.

A broom leans close, gives me a nudge,
Says, 'Come on now, let's not begrudge!'
Together we'll sweep the silly strife,
And laugh at this quaint, chaotic life.

So here we sit—an odd parade,
In a room where charades won't fade.
I'll toast the mundane of the day,
With my half-filled coffee cup of play!

Footsteps in the Silent Void

I walk on tips, as quiet as a mouse,
Through the nooks of our wonky house.
Each creak and crackle starts to tease,
The floorboards laugh, bending at the knees.

The hallway stretches, like a long salad,
Where shadows gather, their tales valid.
A ghost in slippers gives a wink,
While I tiptoe past that sink.

Mismatched socks in the corner blink,
Reduce their game to a silly wink.
As I detour past the laundry room,
Wishing the basket held fewer gloom.

And so, my feet tread paths unknown,
In a land of giggles, hearts grown.
Between the walls of silence, I hop,
Where silliness lingers and won't stop!

Crooked Corners of Existence

In crooked corners, the dust can spin,
Whirling tales where life begins.
A chair's got stories twisted tight,
Bouncing with laughter through the night.

An old broom leans against the wall,
Dreaming of rocks and great carnival.
While a clock giggles at past events,
Ticking away like a jester's hints.

The mirror winks, full of sass,
Reflecting a dance from the past.
But smiles can bend, like the chairs that creak,
In this lovely mess, I find what I seek.

So here I stand, in a wobbling cheer,
In rooms that echo laughter's leer.
Where every turn holds joy and sass,
We'll toast to the quirks as moments pass!

Fragments of Time and Space

In the hallway, socks take flight,
Chasing shadows, lost in light.
The cat observes with a quizzical gaze,
As toys perform in a dizzying blaze.

Between the kitchen and the den,
Procrastination is my best friend.
A snack attack and then a break,
For every decision, there's a cake.

On one wall hangs a calendar bold,
Yet here I stand, stuck in the fold.
Double check if I've brushed my hair,
Or have I just stumbled into despair?

The microwave hums its gentle song,
While I wonder where the hours have gone.
Rediscovering crumbs, I take a bite,
Turns out snacking is pure delight!

The Dance of Duality

In the living room, rhythms collide,
A dance of slippers, I can't hide.
Left foot waltzes, the right foot fails,
While the pizza delivery guy tells his tales.

Between the couch and shelves of books,
I juggle laundry with hopeful looks.
One sock in the war, the other has fled,
Making the bed—where's the spread?

A call from the fridge, it beckons me close,
Only to find things I don't want to rouse.
A half-empty jar of pickles and cheese,
In this great debate, I simply tease.

With mismatched shoes, I'm off to restart,
One foot in chaos, the other in art.
Living in jest, laughter's my muse,
In tandem we twirl, with nothing to lose!

Solitude in the Sanctuary

In a nook where quiet likes to dwell,
Tea brews in a fitting ceramic shell.
My thoughts parade, in playful retreat,
While rogue dust bunnies conspire at my feet.

From the summit of the desk's great height,
I watch the clock inch under the light.
With every tick, my focus wanes,
As my notebook fills with doodled trains.

In solitude, I'm never alone,
With comic strips as my co-cone.
The fridge whispers secrets of meals not made,
While the washing machine takes a jolly cascade.

Embracing the chaos, I chuckle and sigh,
Where antics of daily woes simply fly.
A sanctuary found in mismatched delight,
Comedians unite in the glow of the night!

The Halfway Haven

In this haven where socks play hide and seek,
I ponder if balancing acts are mystique.
A phone call comes, laughter erupts,
As a cat knocks over the cup that I cupped.

Sipping coffee, I glance at the clock,
It seems to mock me, stones on the dock.
Halfway to nowhere, yet halfway to bliss,
I take a moment, ignore a to-do list.

Here I juggle chores with a pronounced flair,
While dodging a mountain of lint in my chair.
Life's a circus, and I'm in the ring,
With jokes on standby, just waiting to swing!

Embracing the journey, I find my own beat,
Between the kitchen and hall, I'm never discreet.
In this amusing maze, I find my own tune,
Dancing through life, morning, night, and noon!

Reflections in the Half-Light

In the hallway, shadows dance,
Sneaky smiles, a wistful glance.
A game of hide-and-seek we play,
In this quirky, light-lit fray.

Mirrors showing more than face,
Capture laughter, time and space.
It seems the walls are quite the spies,
With secrets held, and playful sighs.

Footsteps echo off the tiles,
Competing with the air-filled smiles.
Who knew a corner could delight,
In all this silly half-light?

We trip on rugs, we giggle loud,
In this house, we stand so proud.
Every room a stage, it seems,
For our most whimsical dreams.

Uncharted Areas of the Heart

In the nook where junk collects,
Hearts beat strange, defy the specs.
Old letters flutter, memories rise,
In this chaos, love's disguise.

Underneath the stacks of clothes,
Lies a treasure, who really knows?
A half-filled jar, of dreams unmet,
Each whimsy, a heart's duet.

Between the laughter and the fuss,
We find joy in the curious fuss.
A hidden note spills out a rhyme,
Telling tales of love and time.

Tangled whispers, secrets shared,
In these corners, hilarity dared.
A heart's compass, going berserk,
Finding home in offbeat work.

The Unseen Passage

Behind the curtain, life unfolds,
Adventures waiting, never told.
With a wink, the portal glows,
What will happen? No one knows!

Staircases turn to slides of fun,
Chasing daylight, on the run.
With each step, we find the jest,
In laughter's grip, we feel the zest.

Doors that squeak, secrets whisper,
Moments freeze, as echoes glimmer.
A hop, a skip, a leap through time,
The absurdity, pure and prime.

We dance through worlds, unseen, unchaste,
In mischief's grip, life won't go to waste.
Each unseen passage leads us home,
In wild escapades, we roam.

Footsteps on Forgotten Floors

On floors that creak with tales unsung,
We leave our laughter, bright and young.
Dusty echoes, a playful sound,
In tight-knit circles, joy is found.

Each step we take, a venture bold,
In corners where stories unfold.
Faded memories slip and slide,
With clumsy grins, we cannot hide.

The tumbles, trips, and silly falls,
Make this space feel like our halls.
Every mark, a badge of glee,
Adventures shared, just you and me.

So let's embrace the odd and strange,
In forgotten rooms, life will change.
Footsteps echo, laughter endures,
In these whimsical, wondrous floors.

The Area of Uncertainty

In the space where socks might hide,
I question if I'm gaining pride.
Do I need a map to find my way,
Or just accept that I'm here to stay?

The fridge is full, yet food's a myth,
That one leftover? A little pith.
Doorways lead to places unseen,
Like a wild party where no one's been.

Sweaters pile high, a tower of woes,
Do I need them all? Who really knows?
I dance with dust bunnies in the night,
In this carnival of endless delight.

Where does that remote go? A quest to find,
Between the couch cushions, peace of mind.
A kingdom built of snacks and drinks,
In this odd realm, one often thinks.

Shadows in the Doorway

A dance of shadows in the hall,
They giggle and whisper, oh what a brawl!
One foot in, one foot out, a silly charade,
Do we step forward, or stay in this shade?

Beware of the laundry, a mountain so grand,
Clothing rebels, can't take a stand.
They plot their revenge, it's all in good fun,
Struggling to keep track of who's won.

The family pets stake their claims with a sigh,
On plush cushions where they've learned to lie.
They watch the world from their cozy perches,
While we get lost in our silly searches.

Are we here or just ghosts, merging in the light?
Do we trip on the threshold of day and night?
In this playful limbo, join the parade,
Where every little mishap is joyfully made.

Halfway Home

I'm halfway home, a curious plight,
With mismatched shoes, I roam tonight.
Is that my jacket on the chair?
Or did it escape in the open air?

The clock ticks loudly, what time is it now?
I'm late for the party, but I'll take a bow.
With an empty plate and a flower in hand,
I saunter in like I've got a grand plan.

Chairs seem to giggle, they dance in a row,
Each with a story they secretly know.
As I navigate through the clutter and throng,
Laughter spills over, where can I belong?

Halfway home, through a window I peek,
Neighbors are chatting, just feeling the week.
In this wacky world of a jumbled frame,
We giggle together, we're all just the same.

Rooms of Distant Dreams

In rooms where dreams play hide and seek,
They whisper softly, so to speak.
A tapestry woven with laughter and cheer,
Every door opened brings in a new sphere.

The cat thinks she rules every chair,
With a flick of her tail, she gives you a scare.
While crumbs gather under the table we know,
That life's little secrets wait for a show.

Textures of pillows, a fort of delight,
Where imaginary castles heighten the night.
We wear crowns of giggles, a wondrous decree,
As we rule over worlds made from glee.

Oh, the mischief found in the corners of time,
In each little space, we make things sublime.
With a wink to the shadows, come join our spree,
In these rooms of dreams, we dance wild and free.

Fables of the Threshold

A sock draped on the chair, a shoe on the floor,
Dust bunnies gathering, oh what a chore!
Half in the kitchen, the other in dreams,
Where's the lost remotes? Life's never as it seems.

The fridge hums a tune, the oven's on break,
A chair sings a song, but oh, what a fake!
Two rooms in a dance, a waltz with a twist,
While the cat takes a leap, I'm lost in the mist.

With laundry as my partner, I tango with clothes,
One sock on the left and the other, who knows?
In the hallway, I trip over stories untold,
In this space of confusion, humor unfolds.

Do I go left for the bathroom? Or right to the hall?
Each step like a riddle, I laugh as I stall.
Life's odd little pages are filled with a grin,
Here's to the chaos that keeps us all in!

The Pause Between Beats

The clock ticks a rhythm, my coffee's gone cold,
I sway in the silence, too funny to hold.
Do I dance in the kitchen or spin on a chair?
Caught in the moment, but do I really care?

The TV's on mute, it's a show without sound,
I'm the comic relief, in my own battleground.
With naps in the lounge, and dreams in the hall,
I'm the jester of space, but who sees my fall?

The dog gives a bark, as if to remind,
That life's just a game, and I'm stuck in a bind.
Do I bounce on the sofa, or skip on the rug?
Every action a punchline, I give it a hug.

With snacks in my pockets and giggles in air,
Every leap from the couch feels like a dare.
Between beats of laughter, I find my own tune,
Life's just a play, under the light of the moon!

Secrets in the Airspace

Whispers of dust float high in the room,
A spider spins tales while avoiding the broom.
The ceiling's a kingdom where shadows do play,
Secrets of corners that dance as they sway.

I hear the fridge gossiping late in the night,
While the toaster's complaining, it's losing a fight.
In the midst of the banter, I chuckle and grin,
What tales could unfold where the air feels thin?

The cat stares at nothing, a ghost in the air,
I join in the laughter, how strange is this affair?
A flicker of whimsy, a peek at the light,
In the antics of spaces, the world's a delight.

With echoes of giggles and sighs of the past,
In this realm of the odd, the moments are vast.
We chase little secrets, beneath the old fan,
In the lighter side of life, humor can span!

Windows to the Unseen

A curtain asks questions, peeking at the street,
Sipping on sunlight, oh what a treat!
Through panes of illusions, adventures await,
While I sip on my tea, life's laughter can't wait.

The garden's a stage for squirrels in a race,
While birds chirp a tune, each flapping with grace.
A door creaks and chuckles as if it knows best,
Every window's a portal for joy manifest.

In the crack of the frame lies a world upside down,
With shadows of kittens who refuse to wear crowns.
These frames frame my moments, clear but offbeat,
In the dance of the day, my heart finds its feet.

So let the world wander, let the wild things roam,
Through laughter and kinks, this space feels like home.
With windows wide open, the view's never mean,
Life's comedy shows through what can't be seen!

This Place We Call 'Between'

In a space that's oddly wide,
I trip on socks that choose to hide.
The walls stand still, they never budge,
While I debate, should I or shouldn't I judge?

A fridge with snacks, a treasure trove,
Yet I can't recall where I stowed.
Chairs that squeak, a floor that creaks,
Life here is just full of peaks!

Sometimes I wonder, how did I land?
In this in-between, life feels unplanned.
I laugh at the quirks, the mishaps too,
This realm of oddities, is it just for a few?

But in this space, there's laughter and cheer,
A joy in the chaos, a moment to steer.
So here's to the place that holds the in-betweens,
With life's little quirks and all its routines.

A Breath in the Suspension

Caught in a pause, just like a game,
Time flickers here, feels a bit insane.
On cue, the doorbell rings out of tune,
A ghost in this limbo hums a funny tune.

The cats plot heists on the window sill,
While I reach for snacks, my belly to fill.
I juggle chores, like a circus show,
In this pause, anything can go!

Hats and coats draped on chairs like art,
Every little detail a quirky part.
And though it's messy, I can't complain,
In this breath, there's humor to gain!

Wipe the dust off my collection of dreams,
Where every mishap is better than it seems.
A laugh in the silence, a pause in the jest,
In this silent place, I feel most blessed.

Frayed Edges of Familiarity

Here I sit on the edge of the known,
Where socks mate wildly, yet I am alone.
Chasing the crumbs that fall from my snack,
In this corner, there's no going back.

The couch holds secrets, of naps and of dreams,
A cushion that talks, or so it seems.
Staring blankly at a wall of 'why?',
Do I belong here, or should I fly?

Each box tells tales of a life's little quirks,
In this oddity, everyone smirks.
With laughter hidden in shadows and light,
I navigate this space, what a delightful sight!

So here's to the mishaps, to each little mess,
To the fumbles and tumbles, I must confess.
In the frayed edges, I find my delight,
In this clever chaos, it all feels right!

Echoes of Untold Stories

In whispers and echoes, tales unfold,
Of socks in pairs that daringly scold.
Each closet holds secrets, laughter, and cries,
In this clever maze, one never complies.

Footsteps tread lightly on scattered old shoes,
A maze of adventures I can't really lose.
I chuckle at ghosts who hover around,
With tales's intertwining, both lost and found.

The furniture grins in a warm embrace,
With history nestled in this cozy space.
Odd hats hang low, sharing their flair,
In these echoes, I find joy to spare.

So let's raise a glass to untold lore,
In this charming realm, there's always much more.
With each clumsy step, we gather and weave,
In the laughter of echoes, all we believe!

Emptiness and Existence

In a room where dust collects,
I ponder what on Earth connects.
My cat thinks it's a grand parade,
While I just sit and slowly fade.

The fridge hums like a lonely tune,
Full of leftovers—dinner's boon.
A dance of forks and spoons at play,
As I wonder if I should eat today.

A chair beside is always bare,
And in my mind, it's quite unfair.
I tell it jokes; it laughs, I'm sure,
But chairs can't talk—of this I'm pure.

Echoes bounce off barren walls,
As I prepare for one of my falls.
Laughter spills in strange forms and fiends,
Where emptiness boasts of untold dreams.

Beneath the Surface of Rooms

Beneath the rugs, the dust bunnies play,
Can't find my socks; they've run away.
A mystery unfolds as I seek,
Adventures in odd corners, so bleak.

The lampshade's puzzled; it winks at me,
While shadows argue on the dark sea.
A battle of light and night's goofy grin,
In this room where chaos wears thin.

The laundry piles like a mountain high,
Each sock a hero that won't die.
They tell tales of pairings gone wrong,
While I snicker and sing a song.

Under the table, the echoes dwell,
With crumbs that whisper their own sweet spell.
Rooms are funny in their own right,
Where silence hums, and chaos takes flight.

In the Space of Shadows

In the shadows, I hide my snack,
As the couch cushions give me flack.
"Drop the chips!" they seem to scream,
While I munch away on my salty dream.

A blanket fort, my fortress tall,
Where I can giggle and never fall.
The ceiling fan spins tales of flight,
As I plot my next snack attack tonight.

The clock's hands mock my lazy ways,
Time drips slowly in this haze.
I glance at the world through the glass,
Wondering if I should let life pass.

Jokes unfurl like laundry lines,
Hanging stories, twisting signs.
In the space where shadows play,
I find humor in another day.

The Threshold of Echoes

At the door, I hear whispers call,
My shoes lie stacked, forming a wall.
They plot escape, I swear it's true,
To steal away and get a view.

I step outside, then quickly in,
Hugging my coffee like a kin.
The echo of footsteps makes me grin,
As I ponder my awkward spin.

The mirror reflects a face perplexed,
A daily show—what's come next?
While socks get lost in their own domain,
I salute them both—those heroes mundane.

In corridors where laughter blends,
Life's sweet humor never ends.
At the threshold, I plot and scheme,
In the echoes, I dare to dream.

The Light That Lingers

A sock on the chair, what a sight,
It dances alone, like a bird in flight.
The sun peeks in, with a cheeky grin,
Lighting up the dust, where mischief begins.

A cat on the shelf, with a royal air,
Pretends to be serious, but doesn't care.
Chasing shadows, in a game of catch,
While I sip my tea, with a quirky patch.

The toast pops up, a sudden cheer,
It jumps like it knows, I'm waiting here.
The walls are painted with stories untold,
But they giggle and whisper, never too bold.

A light that lingers, a mischievous tease,
Whispers of laughter, rides the evening breeze.
I chuckle at moments, so oddly sublime,
In this house full of quirks, I'm having a time.

The Spaces We Create

A chair for my thoughts, a couch for my dreams,
Each corner is bursting with laughter and schemes.
A broom in the corner, a partner in crime,
It knows all my secrets and dances in rhyme.

The fridge hums a tune, in the late afternoon,
Offering snacks, like a friendly cartoon.
I rummage for treasures, the leftovers sing,
In this realm of delight, food's the real king.

There's a rug with a story, woven with cheer,
It hides quite well, all the crumbs from last year.
Yet I tap dance around, in my joyful spree,
With every twirl, it whispers back to me.

Spaces hold laughter, and echoes of play,
As I step through the rooms, in a whimsical way.
With a wink to the light, that streams from above,
These spaces are magic, filled up with love.

The Unwritten Chapters

Books stack like towers, in a comical plight,
Waiting for stories to spill out at night.
An open page beckons, with hopes so grand,
But the pencil just giggles, and won't take a stand.

The dog snores a tune, a gentle serenade,
While dust bunnies plot their grand escapade.
Plotting their escape, from the corners they hide,
Is this just a story? Or reality's ride?

Post-its and doodles, on the fridge they cling,
Reminders of moments, the joys that they bring.
A canvas of laughter, colors so bright,
Hints of my life, in the soft morning light.

The chapters I write, unfold in a mess,
Each page filled with joy, never with stress.
In unwritten tales, I find my delight,
In the quirky adventures that sprout every night.

Dreaming in the Void

The bed squeaks a song, that echoes through time,
While pillows conspire, in a sudsy rhyme.
Blankets are monsters, dressed up for the game,
As I drift into dreams, where nothing is tame.

A clock ticks in jest, with a wink and a chime,
It laughs at my naps, a thieving of time.
The moon plays peek-a-boo, through the swaying trees,
Bringing tales of whimsy, with a fluttering breeze.

In the silence of night, maybe aliens chat,
Discussing our habits, and why we wear that.
Whispers of worlds that we cannot ignore,
As I dance through the void, always wanting more.

Dreaming in the void, with a breakfast surprise,
Pancakes and laughter, beneath open skies.
For every wild thought, there's joy to explore,
In this garden of winks, I long to restore.

www.ingramcontent.com/pod-product-compliance
Lightning Source LLC
Chambersburg PA
CBHW051731290426
43661CB00122B/233